W9-ANN-602

EDGE BOOKS™

WILD ABOUT SNAKES

BOA CONSTRICTORS

BY MELANIE A. HOWARD

Consultants:
Joe Maierhauser, President/CEO
Terry Phillip, Curator of Reptiles

Edge Books are published by Capstone Press,
151 Good Counsel Drive, P.O. Box 669, Mankato, Minnesota 56002.
www.capstonepub.com

Library of Congress Cataloging-in-Publication Data
Howard, Melanie A.
  Boa constrictors / by Melanie A. Howard.
     p. cm.—(Edge books. Wild about snakes)
  Includes index.
  ISBN 978-1-4296-6011-2 (library binding)
  ISBN 978-1-4296-7283-2 (paperback)
  1. Boa constrictor—Juvenile literature. I. Title.
  QL666.O63H69 2012
  597.96'2—dc22   2011010181

Editorial Credits
Brenda Haugen, editor; Ted Williams, designer; Eric Manske, production
specialist

Photo Credits
Alamy: blickwinkel/Schmidbauer, cover, Joe Blossom, 6, 16, 5; AnimalsAnimals:
McDonald Wildlife Photography, 19, 20; Dreamstime: David Gartland, 14; Getty
Images Inc.: Minden Pictures/Pete Oxford, 8, 25; iStockphoto: Denny Medley, 27;
Nature Picture Library: Ross Couper-Johnston, 11; Photo Researchers, Inc: Martin
Wendler, 28, Paul Whitten, 22; Shutterstock: Audrey Snider-Bell, 13, fivespots, 1

Artistic Effects
Shutterstock: Marilyn Volan

TABLE OF CONTENTS

Chapter 1

LARGER THAN LIFE!

Since ancient times people have believed a lot of wild things about boa constrictors. Pliny the Elder wrote that that the body of a child was found in a snake's stomach in AD 77 in Italy. The large snake was called a boa.

In the 600s Isadore of Seville wrote about boas killing herds of oxen. The snake was said to latch on to an ox's or cow's udder, drain the animal's milk, and kill it. The word *boa* even means ox killer.

Just Scary Stories

No snakes like the boa ever existed. But the tales did give Swedish scientist Carl Linnaeus an idea. He decided to name a real group of snakes *Boa* in 1758. Boa constrictors and anacondas are among the snakes that belong to this family.

There are many tales about man-eating boas. Boa constrictors don't eat humans. Yet that hasn't stopped people from making up scary stories about them. Even today a popular poem by Shel Silverstein called "Boa Constrictor" tells of a boa constrictor swallowing a person.

The Real Deal

Boa constrictors are large **reptiles**. Many people keep them as pets. Most owners say boa constrictors are among the easiest snakes to have as pets. They can be picked up and held. They can be fed dead rats.

reptile–a cold-blooded animal that breathes air and has a backbone; most reptiles lay eggs and have scaly skin

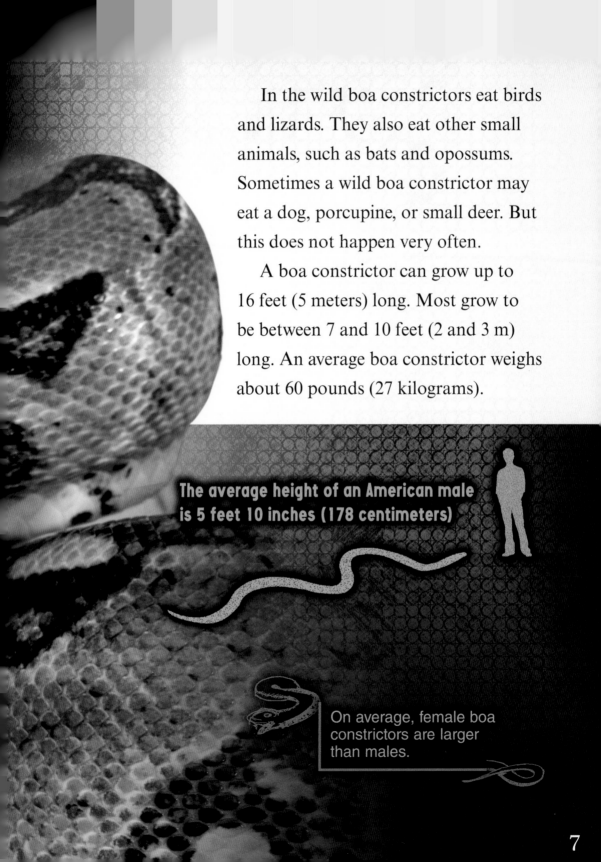

In the wild boa constrictors eat birds and lizards. They also eat other small animals, such as bats and opossums. Sometimes a wild boa constrictor may eat a dog, porcupine, or small deer. But this does not happen very often.

A boa constrictor can grow up to 16 feet (5 meters) long. Most grow to be between 7 and 10 feet (2 and 3 m) long. An average boa constrictor weighs about 60 pounds (27 kilograms).

The average height of an American male is 5 feet 10 inches (178 centimeters)

On average, female boa constrictors are larger than males.

Can You See Me?

Boa constrictors can be found in both North America and South America. They live as far south as Argentina and as far north as northern Mexico. Some boa constrictors live on coastal and Caribbean islands.

Boa constrictors live in rain forests, grasslands, and woodlands. They also live on farmland and **semideserts**. Often they are found by streams and rivers. A boa constrictor may make its home in a hole in the ground made by another animal.

semidesert—an area that is like a desert but gets more rainfall during the year

Boa Constrictor Range

☐ where boa constrictors live

North America

Europe

Asia

Africa

South America

Australia

Antarctica

N W E S

Boa constrictors live and hunt in trees and on the ground. They can grip things by wrapping their tails around them. This allows the snakes to live in tree branches. Young boa constrictors are more likely to live in trees than older boas. The younger snakes are smaller and lighter. They also need more protection from predators.

Most scientists agree that there are about nine types of boa constrictors. The Columbian or common boa is the most well known. Another large group of boa constrictor is the imperial, or Central American, boa.

One of the most unusual boa constrictors is the Argentine boa constrictor. It has a fuzzy white pattern of large spots on its body. The Argentine boa constrictor is the only boa constrictor that is **endangered**.

People who own boa constrictors as pets sometimes have names for specific kinds of boa constrictor, such as "red-tailed boa." These names usually relate to the boa's appearance. They help to identify boa constrictors in the pet trade. But these are not scientific names for the various boa **species**.

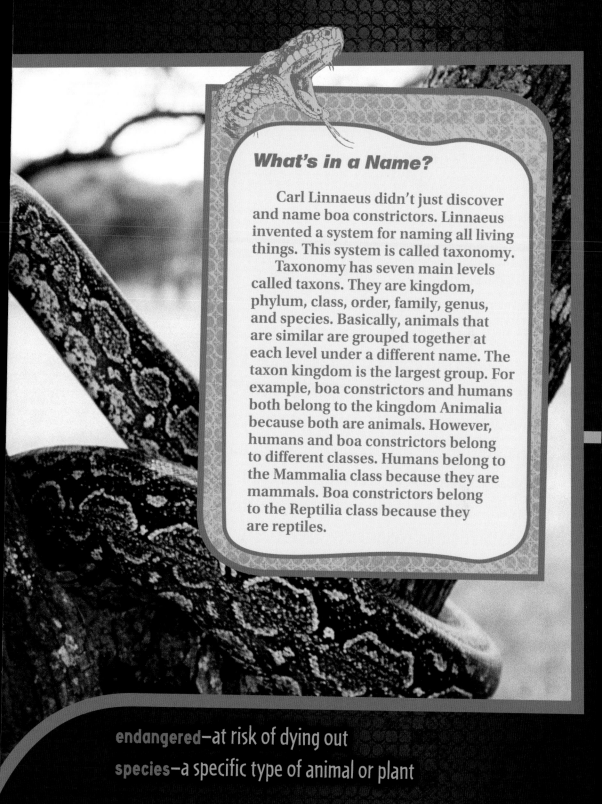

What's in a Name?

Carl Linnaeus didn't just discover and name boa constrictors. Linnaeus invented a system for naming all living things. This system is called taxonomy.

Taxonomy has seven main levels called taxons. They are kingdom, phylum, class, order, family, genus, and species. Basically, animals that are similar are grouped together at each level under a different name. The taxon kingdom is the largest group. For example, boa constrictors and humans both belong to the kingdom Animalia because both are animals. However, humans and boa constrictors belong to different classes. Humans belong to the Mammalia class because they are mammals. Boa constrictors belong to the Reptilia class because they are reptiles.

endangered–at risk of dying out

species–a specific type of animal or plant

Spots and Stripes

One of the most unusual features of a boa constrictor is the pattern on its skin. It has dark, saddle-shaped bands along its cream or brown body. Some boa constrictors appear almost black. However, the unique saddle-shaped markings on their bodies prove them to be boa constrictors.

A boa constrictor has three stripes on its head. One starts at its nose and runs down the middle of its head. Two are on the sides of the head and go through the eyes. The stripes on the sides of a boa constrictor's head form a dark triangle in front of and behind its eyes.

The most recently discovered type of boa constrictor is the long-tailed boa. Most boa constrictors have tails that are about 11 percent of their total body lengths. The male long-tailed boa's tail is more than 14 percent of its total body length.

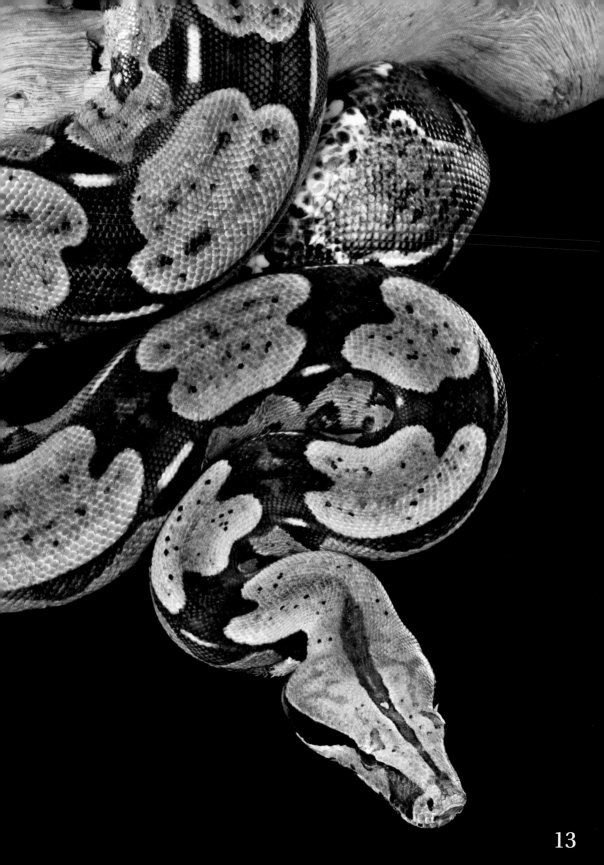

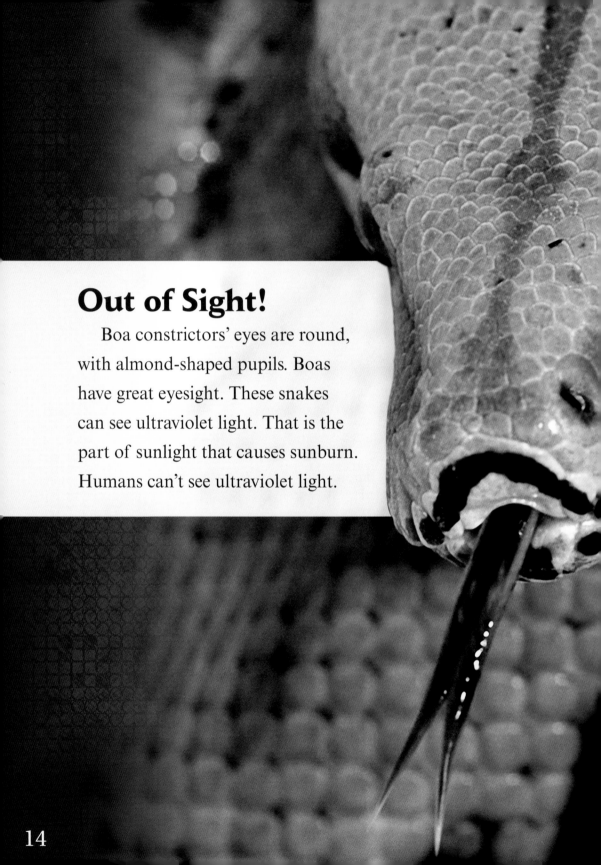

Out of Sight!

Boa constrictors' eyes are round, with almond-shaped pupils. Boas have great eyesight. These snakes can see ultraviolet light. That is the part of sunlight that causes sunburn. Humans can't see ultraviolet light.

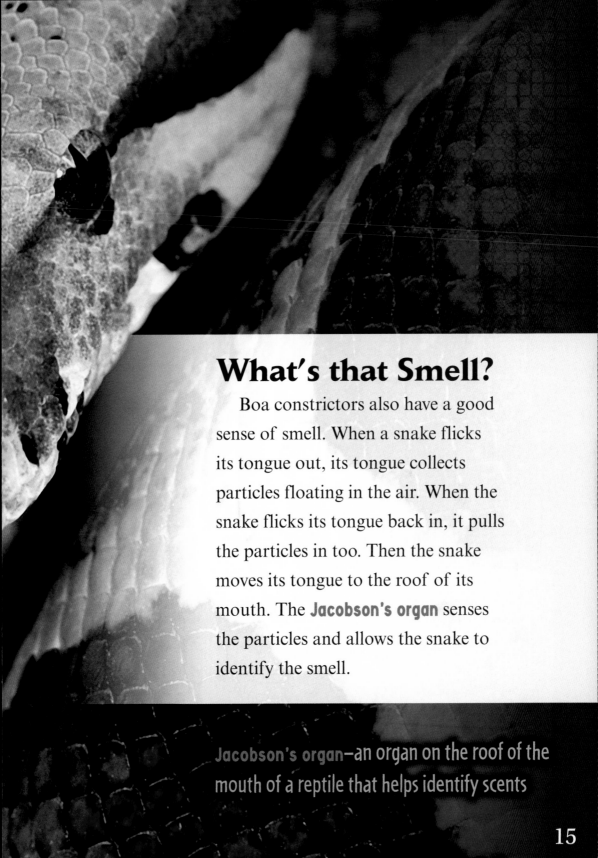

What's that Smell?

Boa constrictors also have a good sense of smell. When a snake flicks its tongue out, its tongue collects particles floating in the air. When the snake flicks its tongue back in, it pulls the particles in too. Then the snake moves its tongue to the roof of its mouth. The **Jacobson's organ** senses the particles and allows the snake to identify the smell.

Jacobson's organ—an organ on the roof of the mouth of a reptile that helps identify scents

15

Other Senses

When an animal moves, it creates a vibration. Boa constrictors can sense vibrations in the ground and in the air through their jaw bones and inner ear bones. These vibrations help alert a boa when a meal or a predator is nearby.

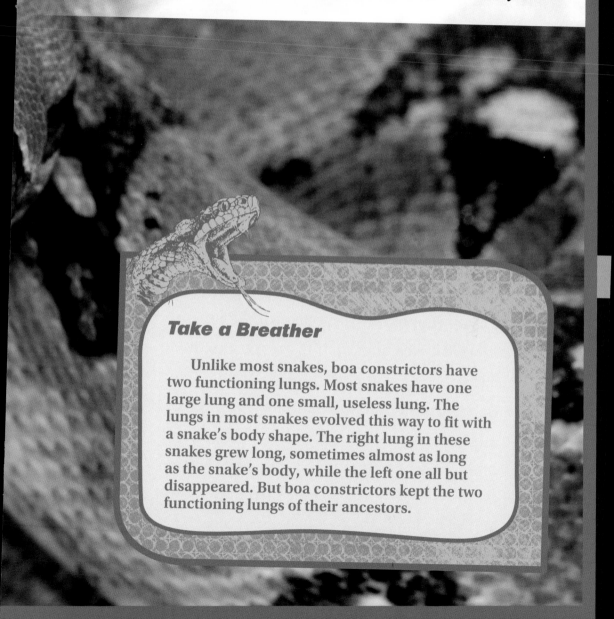

A boa constrictor has heat-sensing pits along the edge of its mouth. With these pits, a snake can sense heat coming off another animal's body.

Take a Breather

Unlike most snakes, boa constrictors have two functioning lungs. Most snakes have one large lung and one small, useless lung. The lungs in most snakes evolved this way to fit with a snake's body shape. The right lung in these snakes grew long, sometimes almost as long as the snake's body, while the left one all but disappeared. But boa constrictors kept the two functioning lungs of their ancestors.

Chapter 3

CONSTRICTION AND COURTING

A boa constrictor is a heavy, muscular snake. It uses its thick body to kill its **prey**. When it catches its meal, a boa constrictor wraps itself around the animal. Then the snake squeezes its prey until the prey dies. This is called **constriction**. The boa constrictor takes part of its name from the way it kills its prey.

Just Warming Up

Boa constrictors are cold-blooded animals. Their body temperatures change with their surroundings. Boa constrictors are most active in the early evening and at night. They sun themselves during the day. Sunning on a rock or a tree branch allows a boa constrictor to raise its body temperature before it goes hunting. A snake cannot hunt if it is too warm or too cold.

prey–an animal hunted by another animal for food
constriction–the process of squeezing an animal to death

Captive boa constrictors are often given dead prey to eat. They sometimes still constrict the dead prey before they eat it.

Lying in Wait

If it has to, a boa constrictor will search for prey. But the snake would rather lie in a tree or on the ground and wait for prey to wander by. The boa constrictor grabs and holds the prey with its teeth. Then the snake coils its body around the prey. After constricting its prey, the snake will eat the animal headfirst.

Boas move in straight lines at about 1 mile (1.6 kilometers) per hour.

A boa constrictor has flexible jaws. The jaws allow the snake to swallow prey bigger than its own head. The lower jaw has two parts that meet in the middle. These parts can separate allowing the snake to open its mouth wide. The two parts of the lower jaw can also move on their own. This helps the snake push the prey down its throat.

A boa constrictor has rows of hooked teeth that are curved toward the snake's throat. These hooked teeth help direct prey down the snake's throat as it is swallowing. When a tooth breaks, a new one grows to take its place.

It takes a boa constrictor four to six days to **digest** its prey. If it eats something big, a boa constrictor may wait several weeks before having to eat again.

Mating Season

Boa constrictors are old enough to mate when they are about 3 years old. They usually mate between April and August, but mating season can vary by region.

During mating season male boa constrictors seek out females. Since most boa constrictors live alone, males may travel great distances to find females.

A female boa is usually pregnant between five and eight months before giving birth. Boa constrictors give birth to live young. On average, a boa constrictor gives birth to about 25 young at a time. However, a female can give birth to as many as 80 young.

Young boa constrictors are on their own from birth. They are born knowing how to hunt and to hide. Yet they don't all survive. Some animals prey on the young snakes, including hawks and wild pigs.

Home Sweet Home

The island of Dominica, in the Caribbean Sea, is home to the only boa constrictors known to live in groups. Dominican or clouded boa constrictors sometimes share dens with others of their kind.

Boa constrictors are popular as pets. Some types of boa constrictors suffer because too many are being taken from the wild. The Convention on International Trade in Endangered Species of Wild Fauna and Flora (CITES) keeps a list of endangered and **protected** species. The Argentine boa constrictor has endangered status on this list. All other boas, not just boa constrictors, are considered protected on this list.

All the nations that are members of CITES are committed to protecting the animals on the list. Many laws have been passed in the United States and other countries about owning and selling animals on the CITES list.

Boa Constrictors as Pets

Boa constrictors sold as pets should be born in **captivity**, not taken from the wild. Captive boa constrictors are more likely to be comfortable around humans than those born in the wild are. Compared to other pets, boas can live a long time. Boas can live more than 20 years in captivity.

Be Prepared

Many people keep boa constrictors as pets. But before you decide to buy one, you should be prepared. Boas need plenty of space. A boa needs a tank at least 6 feet (1.8 m) long, 2 feet (61 centimeters) deep, and 2 feet (61 cm) wide. The snake needs things to climb on that won't break or fall under its weight. A boa could get hurt if it falls or something falls on it. A boa also likes to have somewhere to hide, such as a cardboard box.

A boa needs a large water container for drinking and bathing. Depending on the snake's size, it will eat small mice, rats, or rabbits.

You need to be more careful with a snake than you do with a dog or cat. It could take a while for a snake to be comfortable enough to let you handle it.

captivity—the condition of being kept in a cage

Threats to Boas

Humans pose the biggest threat to wild boa constrictors. Some people kill the snakes and use their skins to make leather items, such as wallets and belts. Boa constrictors are also threatened by vehicles. Many snakes die because they are run over by cars. Some people run over the snakes on purpose.

In some areas people eat boa constrictors. They are also sold in Brazil, Peru, and other South American countries for use as medicines. Some people believe parts of the snake can cure human diseases. There is no proof that any part of a boa constrictor can cure illness, but they are killed for medicine anyway.

Boa constrictors are much more valuable alive. They help keep animal populations in balance. By doing so, the snakes help keep dangerous diseases their prey carries from spreading.

With more understanding, people may learn to respect boa constrictors instead of fear them. The only truly frightening thing about boa constrictors is that we could lose them forever.

Boa constrictors will attack and bite if they feel threatened.

GLOSSARY

captivity (kap-TIV-uht-ee)—the condition of being kept in a cage

constriction (con-STRIK-shun)—the process of squeezing an animal to death

digest (die-JEST)—to break down food so it can be used by the body

endangered (en-DAYN-juhrd)—at risk of dying out

Jacobson's organ (JA-kub-suns OR-gun)—an organ on the roof of the mouth of a reptile that helps identify scents

prey (PRAY)—an animal hunted by another animal for food

protected (proh-TEK-ted)—defended against dying out

reptile (REP-tile)—a cold-blooded animal that breathes air and has a backbone; most reptiles lay eggs and have scaly skin

semidesert (SEM-eye-de-zuhrt)—an area that is like a desert but gets more rainfall during the year

species (SPEE-sheez)—a specific type of animal or plant

READ MORE

Harrison, Paul. *Snakes.* Up Close. New York: PowerKids, 2007.

Menon, Sujatha. *Discover Snakes.* Discover Animals. Berkeley Heights, N.J.: Enslow Pub., 2009.

Stewart, Melissa. *Snakes!* Washington, D.C.: National Geographic, 2009.

INTERNET SITES

FactHound offers a safe, fun way to find Internet sites related to this book. All of the sites on FactHound have been researched by our staff.

Here's all you do:

Visit *www.facthound.com*

Type in this code: 9781429660112

INDEX